Laudate Dominum

Psalm 148

Andrew Carter

for soprano or mezzo-soprano solo, mixed chorus, and orchestra

vocal score

CONTENTS

MUSIC DEPARTMENT

OXFORD
UNIVERSITY PRESS

OXFORD
UNIVERSITY PRESS

Great Clarendon Street, Oxford OX2 6DP, England
198 Madison Avenue, New York, NY10016, USA

Oxford University Press is a department of the University of Oxford.
It furthers the University's aim of excellence in research, scholarship,
and education by publishing worldwide

Oxford is a registered trade mark of Oxford University Press
in the UK and in certain other countries

© Oxford University Press 2001

Database right Oxford University Press (maker)

First published 2001

5 7 9 10 8 6 4

ISBN 0-19-335504-3

Printed and bound in Great Britain by Caligraving Limited

Laudate Dominum was first performed on 22 May 1999 in Oxford Town Hall by Benson Choral
Society and the Elgar Orchestra, conducted by Christopher Walker. Supported by funds from
Southern Arts.

Instrumentation: 2 flutes, 2 oboes, 2 clarinets in Bb and A, 2 bassoons, 2 horns in F,
2 trumpets in Bb, timpani, percussion (2 players), harp, organ (optional), and strings. Full scores and
orchestral material available for hire from the publisher's hire library.

Front cover: Detail of York Minster choir screen, north side. The angel musicians on the lower row,
playing lute or harp, are plasterwork additions by the early nineteenth-century Francesco Burnasconi.
Higher up, their fifteenth-century stone counterparts have a much livelier time with (left to right)
hurdy-gurdy, bagpipes, two shawms, a singer, portative organ, cymbals, and sackbut.
Photographer: Jim Kershaw. Reproduced by kind permision of the Dean and Chapter of York.

Duration: 20 minutes

Commissioned by Benson Choral Society, Oxfordshire to celebrate its Fiftieth Anniversary season in 1999.

Laudate Dominum
Psalm 148

Gallican Psalter

ANDREW CARTER

Duration: 20 minutes

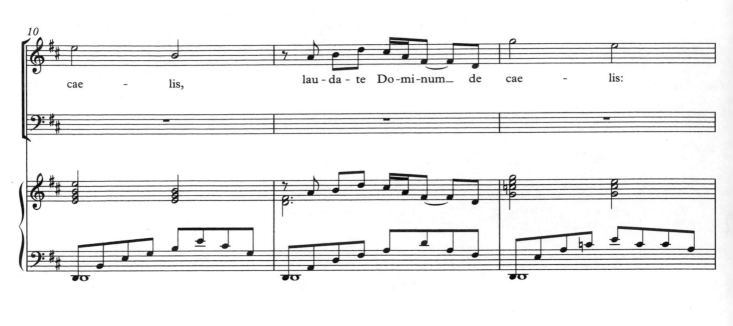

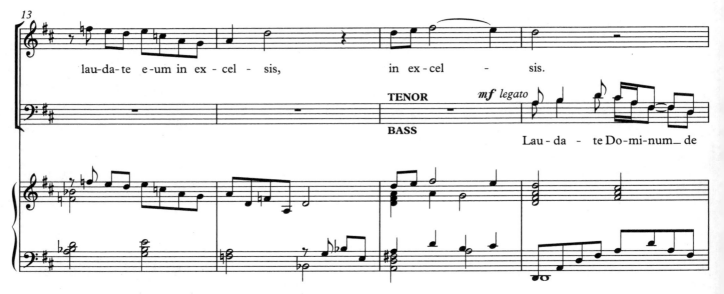

Psalm 148: O praise the Lord of heaven: praise him in the height.

Praise him, all ye angels of his: praise him, all his host.

in ex — cel — sis,_____

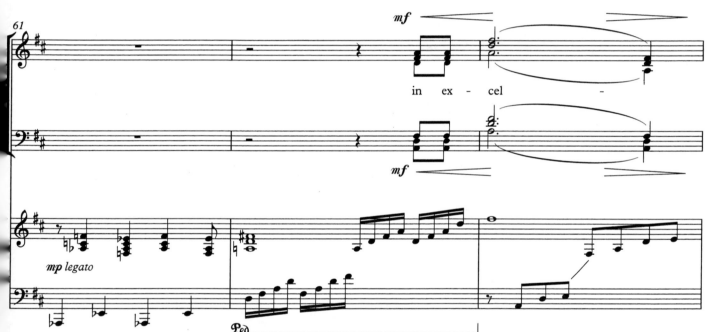

in ex — cel —

- sis.

2. Sol et luna

Praise him, sun and moon:

praise him, all ye stars and light.

Praise him, all ye heavens: and ye waters that are above the heavens.

Let them praise the name of the Lord:

3. Quia ipse dixit

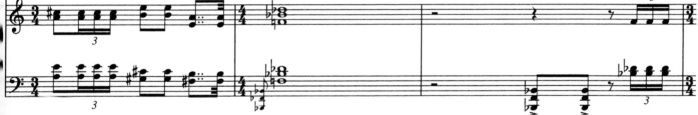

for he spake the word, and they were made; he commanded, and they were created.

He hath made them fast for ever and ever:

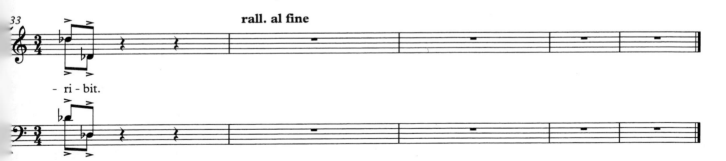

attacca

he hath given them a law which shall not be broken.

4. Laudate Dominum de terra

Praise the Lord upon earth:

attacca

5. Dracones et omnes abyssi

(Praise the Lord) . . . ye dragons, . . .

et om - nes, omnes a - by - ssi,___ lau - da - te Do - mi - num,___

lau - da - te Do - mi - num___ dra - co - nes

et om - nes, omnes a - by - ssi.___

. . . and all deeps;

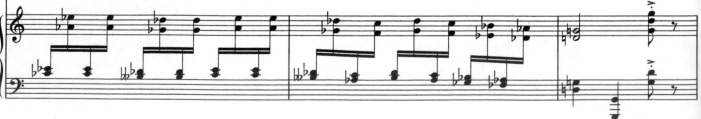

Fire and hail, snow and vapours: wind and storm, . . .

. . . fulfilling his word;

6. Montes et colles

Mountains and all hills: fruitful trees and all cedars;

Beasts and all cattle: worms and feathered fowls; Kings of the earth; . . .

et om-nes po - pu-li: prin-ci-pes et om - nes ju - di-ces ter - rae,

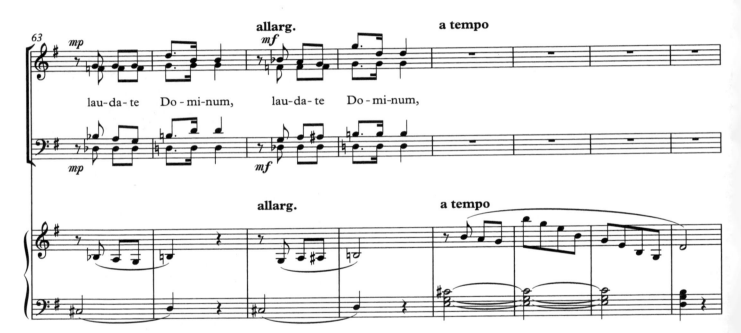

lau-da-te Do - mi-num, lau-da-te Do-mi-num,

lau - da - te Do - mi - num.____

. . . and all people: princes and all judges of the world;

7. Juvenes et virgines

Young men and maidens, old men and children, praise the name of the Lord:

qui - a ex - al - ta - tum est, qui - a ex - al - ta - tum est

for his name only is excellent:

Oboes

Violins

Flutes

Clarinets

K

f

Ju - ve -nes et vir - gi -nes, ju - ve -nes et vir - gi - nes,

poco f

se - nes cum ju - ni - o - ri - bus lau - dent

no - - - - men Do - mi - ni,

f

Do - mi - ni.

ff

attacca

8. Confessio

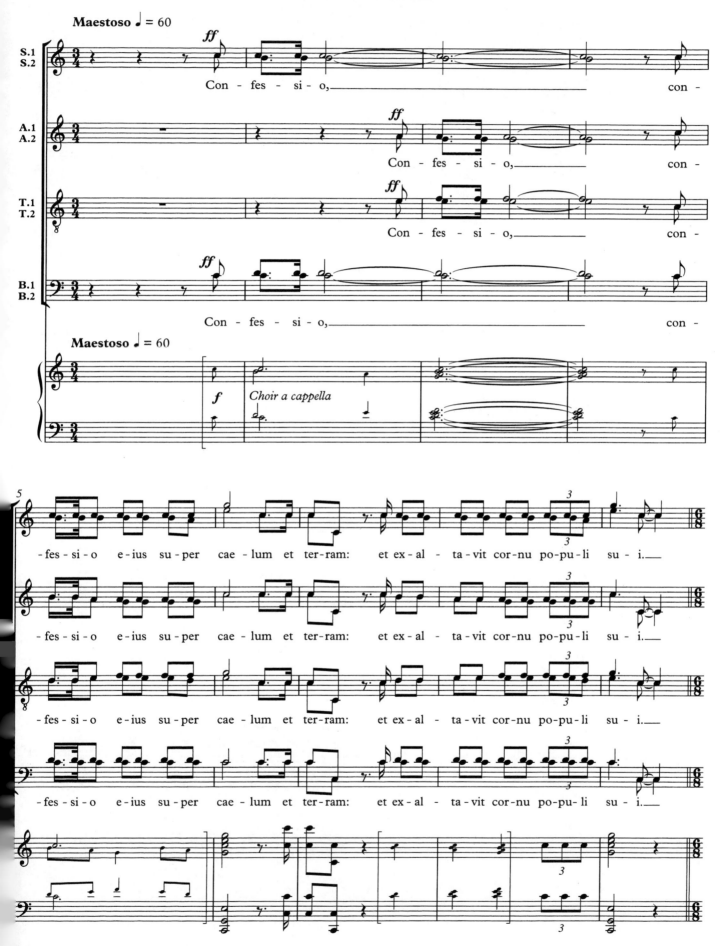

Praise him above heaven and earth: and he shall exalt the horn of his people;

all his saints shall praise him: even the children of Israel, even the people that serveth him.

Glory be to the Father, and to the Son: . . .

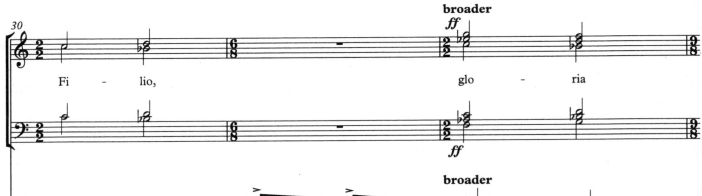

. . . and to the Holy Ghost;

As it was in the beginning, is now, and ever shall be: world without end.

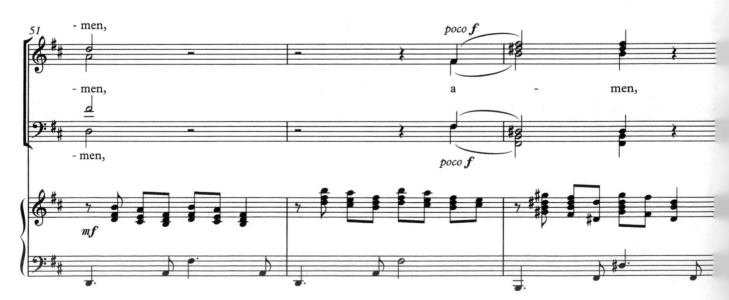

Amen.

a - men,

a - men.

Clarinet

Harp

Bishopthorpe, YORK
9 . xii . 1998

TEXT AND TRANSLATION

Laudate Dominum, Psalm 148

Laudate Dominum de caelis: laudate eum in excelsis.
O praise the Lord of heaven: praise him in the height.
Laudate eum omnes Angeli eius: laudate eum omnes virtutes eius.
Praise him, all ye angels of his: praise him, all his host.

Laudate eum sol et luna: laudate eum omnes stellae et lumen.
Praise him, sun and moon: praise him, all ye stars and light.
Laudate eum caeli caelorum: et aquae omnes quae super caelos sunt, laudent nomen Domini.
Praise him, all ye heavens: and ye waters that are above the heavens. Let them praise the name of the Lord:

Quia ipse dixit, et facta sunt: ipse mandavit, et creata sunt.
for he spake the word, and they were made; he commanded, and they were created.
Statuit ea in aeternum et in saeculum saeculi: praeceptum posuit, et non praeteribit.
He hath made them fast for ever and ever: he hath given them a law which shall not be broken.

Laudate Dominum de terra:
Praise the Lord upon earth:

dracones et omnes abyssi.
ye dragons, and all deeps;
Ignis, grando, nix, glacies, spiritus procellarum: quae faciunt verbum eius:
Fire and hail, snow and vapours: wind and storm, fulfilling his word;

Montes et omnes colles: ligna fructifera et omnes cedri.
Mountains and all hills: fruitful trees and all cedars;
Bestiae et universa pecora: serpentes et volucres pennatae.
Beasts and all cattle: worms and feathered fowls;
Reges terrae et omnes populi: principes et omnes judices terrae.
Kings of the earth and all people: princes and all judges of the world;

Juvenes et virgines, senes cum junioribus laudent nomen Domini: quia exaltatum est nomen eius solius.
Young men and maidens, old men and children, praise the name of the Lord: for his name only is excellent:

Confessio eius super caelum et terram: et exaltavit cornu populi sui.
Praise him above heaven and earth: and he shall exalt the horn of his people;
Hymnus omnibus sanctis eius: filiis Israel, populo appropinquanti sibi.
all his saints shall praise him: even the children of Israel, even the people that serveth him.

Gloria Patri, et Filio, et Spiritui Sancto.
Glory be to the Father, and to the Son: and to the Holy Ghost;
Sicut erat in principio, et nunc, et semper: et in saecula saeculorum. Amen.
As it was in the beginning, is now, and ever shall be: world without end. Amen.

This Latin version of Psalm 148 is from Jerome's *Gallican Psalter*, widely used prior to the early 1960s. The English translation, both here and at the foot of the music, is based on that of the *Book of Common Prayer*.